You can read music

The practical guide by Paul Harris

© 2014 by Paul Harris
All rights administered worldwide by Faber Music Ltd
This edition first published in 2014
Bloomsbury House 74–77 Great Russell Street London WC1B 3DA
Music processed by MacMusic
Text and cover designed by Susan Clarke
CD recorded and produced by Oliver Wedgwood
Printed in England by Caligraving Ltd

ISBN10: 0-571-53845-2
EAN13: 978-0-571-53845-4

To buy Faber Music publications or to find out about the full range of titles available
please contact your local music retailer or Faber Music sales enquiries:
Faber Music Ltd, Burnt Mill, Elizabeth Way, Harlow CM20 2HX
Tel: +44 (0) 1279 82 89 82   Fax: +44 (0) 1279 82 89 83
sales@fabermusic.com   fabermusicstore.com

FABER *ff* MUSIC

Part 1 **Getting started**

Music notation is sound written down

And it's written down in the same way, whether it's for the piano or for a singer, for the cello or clarinet, for the trumpet or tubular bells, for the flute or flugal horn. *Music notation is sound written down.*

Music notation is not code for pressing a key or a valve or for where to place your finger on a fingerboard. It's simply symbols that represent SOUND.

This book is going to help you to understand and make sense of the main symbols we use to represent sound on the written page or, in other words, to *read music*. Do sing all the examples. You may not always be singing in the same vocal range as on the recording (as it will at times be too high or too low for you) but that won't matter.

Here we go …

Alternative US musical terms are given in brackets throughout.

Firstly, a very important point: reading music is not difficult! And to learn to read music you won't need an instrument – just your eyes, your ears (and a CD player or computer), your brain and your voice.

Read the words in the box below and then do what they say:

As soon as you've finished reading these words turn over to the next page ...

You did it. Let's have a think about what you just did.

- *You read the words* – in your head.

- *You heard the words* – in your head.

- *You understood their meaning* – and so you turned the page and are now here reading these words.

Words have two things: sounds and meaning.

We can hear them, say them, write them and READ THEM.

Music is just the same. We can hear music; most of us are probably learning to play or sing music (which is like saying words); we are all capable of learning to write music and…

…we can to learn to read music. It will be as simple as reading these words!

Happy birthday!

It's time to sing *Happy Birthday* (even if it's not your birthday...).
Sing it loudly!

> Each syllable you sang is represented in music by what we call
> a **note**. Here is one: 𝅝
>
> A note represents two things: the **pitch** (how high or low the
> sound is) and **duration** (how long the note lasts). Notes can
> have open middles (white, as above), or be solid black (as
> below).

- The 'py' of *Hap-py* is a shorter note but at the same pitch as the
  Hap. *Birth* is a step higher in pitch than *hap-py*:

Sing: Hap-py birth...

- Notice that step *up* from *py* to *birth*.

- *day* returns to the same pitch as *hap-py*:

Sing: Hap-py birth-day

- *birth*, *day* and *to* are longer notes than *happy*:

Sing: Hap-py   birth - day   to...

- *to* is the highest note of the set. Sing it again and listen to the jump in pitch between *day* and *to*.

- Finally, *you* is the longest note and one step lower than *to*.

Sing: **Hap-py birth - day to you.**

Important words

So now we know some important words involved in reading music: **note** and **pitch**. And for everything that comes under the heading of note **duration** (short or long) we use the word **rhythm**.

I'm counting on you

When we see a note on a page of music we can tell two things: its **pitch** (how high or low it is) and its **duration** (its length in time).

- Using a watch, clock, digital device or **metronome** (set to 60), listen or watch the seconds ticking away and start to feel those seconds.

- Count '1 2 3 4'. Each number = one second.

- Next count: **1** 2 3 4 **1** 2 3 4 **1** 2 3 4 **1** 2 3 4 – again each number for one second, but count **1** louder than the others.

- Tap each number as you count it.

> If we want a note to last for 4 counts we write one that looks like that slightly squashed circle we've already met. It's called a **semibreve** (or **whole note**) and lasts for 4 counts or **beats**: 𝅝

Now to read your first piece of music: four semibreves that last for four beats each. Count aloud and clap on each **1** (the beginning of the note). Make sure all the beats are of equal length:

𝅝   𝅝   𝅝   𝅝

1 2 3 4 **1** 2 3 4 **1** 2 3 4 **1** 2 3 4

Count the four notes again, putting your finger on each note as you begin it. Tap the beats (four for each note), and this time hear each note in your head as a continuous musical sound – any pitch you like, perhaps as 'lah', 'doo' or 'moo'. You've just read some music!

Staves and a cow

Music is written on a **stave**.

Here's an empty stave with no music on it:

A stave is made up of five lines.

> It's important to see the stave is as five separate lines. I find it useful to imagine it like a fence – you would be able to see a cow behind it!

Those five lines are like a ladder. Go up the ladder and the music will get higher – go down it and the music will get lower.

The key to the door

Before we look and hear notes on the stave, there's a symbol we need to learn about. It's called a **clef** (a French word meaning key) and it always sits at the beginning of a stave. There are different clefs, but for the time being we are only going to use one. It's a very elegant symbol called the **treble clef** and it tells us the exact pitch of the notes. Here it is sitting at the beginning of this stave:

It's as easy as A B C (D E F G)

Musical notes are named after the first seven letters of the alphabet. Let's see where the note A lives on the stave and what it looks like written as a four-beat note or **semibreve** (or **whole note**):

- Listen to Track 1 while looking at the note A on the stave above. You'll hear four introductory beats and the A sung for four beats.

- After you've heard the note, continue looking at the stave and *hear the note in your head* (tap the four counts with your hand or foot).

- Still looking at the note (and tapping the counts), sing it for four beats, beginning the note with the sound 'A', as on track 1.

You've just read some more music – rhythm and pitch. And you've read it in your head (reading to yourself) and sung it (reading out loud). That's what reading music is all about.

Time to take your pulse

Here's another word we need to learn: **pulse**. The pulse in music is like your pulse or your heartbeat – it keeps the music alive and moving forwards.

Look at this line of music then do the activities below.

Track 2

- First listen to Track 1 to remind yourself of the A.

- Tap four introductory pulses and then hear the note A ringing strongly in your head for four beats.

- Now, keeping the pulse going, hear the four notes in your head, imagining the syllable 'A' (the letter name of the note) at the beginning of each note.

- Next sing the four notes out loud.

- Finally listen to track 2 to hear the music, pointing to each note as you hear it.

A man walked into a bar (ouch)

To make reading music easier we split the stave into short units called **bars** (or **measures**). Bars can have different numbers of beats in them. We're only going to look at bars with four beats in them for now. To show that, we put a 4 after the clef (this is called a **time signature**) and we indicate the bars by adding **barlines**. Here's that last piece again complete with barlines. Hear it in your head and then sing it, tapping the pulse as you do so. You may want to listen to Track 1 again for the note.

Here's a fun way to get a good feel for the pulse. Instead of tapping the pulse, try walking round the room, one step for each beat. Read the music and sing it as you walk. Try not to bump into anything!

Let's do it again but at a different speed (or tempo). Start tapping a quicker pulse (about two per second) and hear the piece in your head, then sing it. Think about how different it felt compared to the slower version.

More note lengths

We've met the semibreve, which lasts four counts or beats. Here are two more note lengths:

A **minim** (or **half note**) looks like this ♩ and lasts for two counts (or beats).

A **crotchet** (or **quarter note**) looks like this ♩ and is just one count (or beat) long.

These notes are made up of a **notehead** and a **stem**.

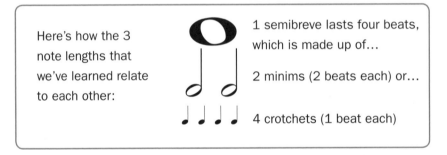

Here's how the 3 note lengths that we've learned relate to each other:

1 semibreve lasts four beats, which is made up of...

2 minims (2 beats each) or...

4 crotchets (1 beat each)

Listen to track 3 and follow the music below. Tap along with the pulse.

Track 3

Pulse:

Still tapping the pulse, hear the piece in your head and then sing it out loud (sing each note to the note name 'A' as on the track).

More notes

So now we know that there are seven different note names and they are named after the first seven letters of the alphabet:

A B C D E F G

These notes are written either on the lines that make up the stave or in the spaces between the lines. After we get to G we begin at A again, like this:

Track 4

As the notes climb up the stave (going up the ladder), they get higher in pitch, and as they go down they get lower in pitch.

Imagine what track 4 might sound like, and then listen to it. Point to each note as you hear it. Notice the first eight notes are going up and the second eight notes are going down. Did it sound like you thought it would?

Music and patterns

As you learn to read music you'll notice that combinations of notes make patterns. Some of these patterns occur over and over again, similar to some very common words like 'the' or 'and' or 'music'.

Here's a common pattern:

Track 6

Track 5 Listen to track 5, which gives the first note, C. Can you hear the whole pattern in your head? Sing it, using the letter name of each note, then listen to it on track 6.

Here are three important facts about that musical pattern:

- Each note was higher than the previous note.

- All the notes were next door to each other.

- Next door notes move from a line to a space or a space to a line.

Going up

Track 6

Hear it in your head again and then sing the pattern.

Now listen to track 6, pointing to each note as it's sung.

Patterns and phrases

Another word to describe a short pattern in music is a phrase.

Here's another common phrase or pattern:

Track 7

Can you see the pattern? It goes up then down. Hear it in your head
before you sing it. (Listen to track 5 for the first note.) Then listen to it
on track 7, pointing to each note as you hear it.

Turn write!

We've been *reading* music, *singing* music and *listening* to music, but
we haven't *written* any so far! Here's an empty stave. Simply copy the
music above. Once you've copied it, hear it internally (in your head),
then sing it from your own handwritten version. (Listen to track 5 for
the first note, C.)

Track 7

You've now written, read and sung the music!

Scales

So, we've learnt that reading music is:

- **seeing** the notes (which tell us both their pitch and length) and at the same time **hearing** those notes internally (in your head) which allows us to

- **sing** those notes aloud (it could be playing them as well, but it's very useful to be able to sing them first).

The notes that make up a tune usually belong to a **scale**. The eight notes of that scale usually form the main building bricks of a piece or song.

C major is often the scale we learn first. That's because on the piano it's made up of white notes only. Here's a scale of C major written in crotchets (one-beat notes). It starts and ends on C. Look at the notes and listen to track 8.

Track 8

Now, reading the music, hear the scale in your head (internally) and then sing it. Each note is one step higher in pitch than the previous note – one step higher on the ladder.

If you have a staircase handy with at least eight steps have a go at this activity: listen to track 5 to hear a C. Stand on the bottom step with this book and sing the C. Now climb the stairs singing the next note on each step. Don't fall over!

Reading short phrases

Here are some short, one-bar phrases all beginning on C, using just crotchets (one-beat notes). Here's what to do for each one:

- Look at the phrase to get a general idea of what it says, then describe it. For example *'the first phrase is the same note repeated four times.'* Look for patterns the notes may make – such as notes which repeat or move up and down.

- Tap four introductory beats, then, continuing to tap, hear the phrase in your head, internally singing each note to its pitch name. (Listen to track 5 for the first note, C.)

- Tap four introductory beats then, continuing to tap, sing the phrase out loud (using the letter names, 'lah' or any sound you like).

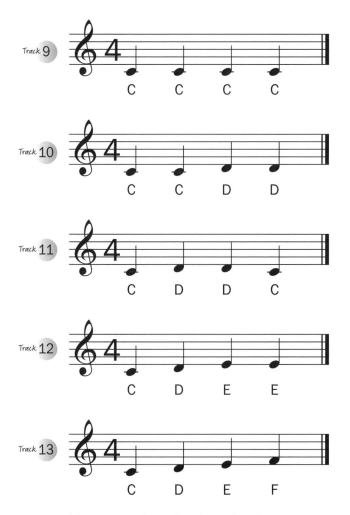

Listen to each track to hear the phrases.

Reading longer phrases

Here are some two-bar phrases all beginning on C, using just crotchets (one-beat notes) and ending with a minim (a two-beat note). This is what to do for each:

- Look at the phrase and get a general idea of it. Look for patterns – notes which repeat or go up and down, for example. Describe it in words.

- Tap four beats of pulse, then, continuing to tap the pulse, hear the phrase in your head, internally singing each note to its pitch name. (Listen to track 5 to hear the first note, C.)

- Continue to tap the pulse and sing the phrase out loud.

Listen to the tracks to hear the phrases, pointing to each note as you hear it.

Be a composer

Have a go at making up your own two-bar phrases. Begin with a
crotchet C and end with a minim C (like the examples above). But
between those notes it's up to you! In your tune, either repeat notes
or move by step to a next-door note. Make sure the notes in each bar
add up to four beats.

Listen to Track 5 for the first note (C), then hear your own piece
internally first and then sing it.

Download more manuscript paper (empty staves) if you find you enjoy
writing your own music (there are a number of websites that provide
free manuscript paper which you can print out).

Reading even longer phrases

Let's try reading some four-bar phrases now.

Prepare each phrase using the instructions on page 18. Sing the notes to their pitch names or 'ah', 'lah', 'doo' or any syllable you like. Listen to each phrase after you've read, heard internally and sung it.

You should feel that you really can read music now. You're able to look at it and understand it – just like reading these words. You can hear the sounds in your head (like you can hear these words in your head) and you can sing the sounds out loud – like reading these words out loud – if you wanted to. It really isn't difficult!

Spot that tune

Let's put your reading to the test! Here are some well-known tunes.
Can you tell what they are just by reading them? Three of them begin
on E and some have small leaps. Listen to tracks 23–26 after you've
read and had a go at recognising each. Keep tapping the pulse while
you hear each tune in your head.

(The answers are on page 64.)

Time for a rest

For each rhythmic note value (so far we've come across crotchets, minims and semibreves) there is an equivalent rest. A rest indicates silence in music. That period of silence is exactly the length of the rest.

- A **crotchet rest** (or **quarter rest**) lasts 1 beat

- A **minim rest** (or **half rest**) lasts 2 beats

- A **semibreve rest** (or **whole rest**) lasts 4 beats (or a whole bar)

Here are the symbols for these rests:

Crotchet rest

Minim rest

Semibreve rest

Here are some tunes that include rests. Prepare to read these tunes
as you have done before:

- Look at the phrase and get a general idea of it; check for patterns
  and describe it in words.

- Tap four beats of pulse, then, continuing to tap the pulse, hear the
  phrase in your head. (Listen to track 5 to hear the first note.)

- Make sure you count and observe the rests.

- Continue to tap the pulse and sing the phrase out loud.

Listen to each tune, pointing to each note or rest as you hear it.

The write time again

Have a go at writing some four-bar phrases. Here is a list of the ingredients you can use:

- The notes C, D, E, F and G

- ♩ and 𝄽

- 𝅗𝅥 and ▬

- 𝅝 and ▬

As it's your music you can write what you like, but, for the moment, stick to these three rules:

- Begin and end on the note C.

- Only use a 𝅝 in the final bar.

- Notes should repeat or move by step to a next-door note.

Try to hear each phrase in your head as you are writing it.

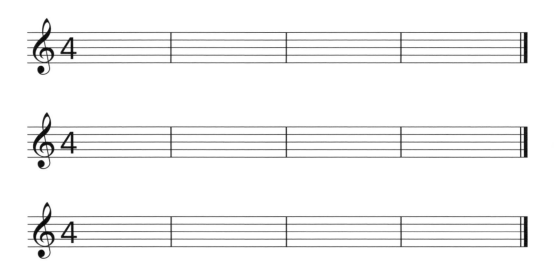

Listen to Track 5 for the first note (C). Tap a pulse then hear each of your tunes internally, and then sing them out loud.

Extending the note range

We're going to add the sixth note of C major to our phrases: the note A.

Listen to track 5 for the note C, then tap one preparatory bar and (continuing to tap the pulse) read this phrase internally:

Try reading (and then singing) this tune backwards! Start at the end and read backwards to the beginning. What do you notice?

Here's a longer tune for you to read. It has all six notes and all three rhythmic values. Tap four introductory beats, then (keeping the pulse going) hear the tune in your head. Track 5 gives you the first note. Next, reading the music, sing it out loud. You may know the tune (see answer on page 64).

Track 32

Now listen to it, pointing to each note as you hear it.

Loud and quiet

Written music can tell us other things as well as the pitch and length of notes. It can tell us how loud or quiet the music should be. There are several different 'volume' markings available, which we call **dynamics**.

> **Dynamics** are usually written just below the notes. They are shown as Italian abbreviations.
>
> Let's start with two:
>
> f (**forte**) which means loud
>
> p (**piano**) which means quiet

Read this tune and hear it with the dynamic markings too. (Set the pulse going first!) Then sing it. Remember to make a big contrast between loud and quiet.

Track 33

A musical jigsaw puzzle

Here are some short one-bar phrases. Decide on what you think would
be a good order to put them together, then copy each bar into your
chosen position in the empty stave below (you don't need to include
the clef each time). Then hear and sing your Jigsaw Tune.

Try another version…

Which version do you prefer? Why?

A leap of faith

Most of our notes have moved by step so far. As you learn more pieces and songs you will come across leaps between notes.

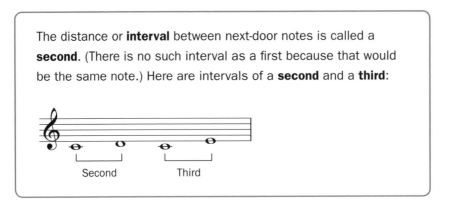

The distance or **interval** between next-door notes is called a **second**. (There is no such interval as a first because that would be the same note.) Here are intervals of a **second** and a **third**:

Second Third

Let's look at some leaps of a third in a tune. In the usual way, read and hear internally, and then sing this phrase (then listen to it):

Track 34

Here's a well-known tune which includes two leaps of a third. Set up a pulse then hear it in your head – do you recognise it? (The answer is on page 64.) Then, keeping the pulse going, sing it aloud – complete with dynamics!

Track 35

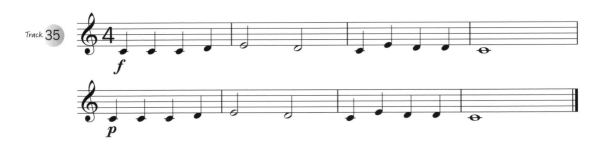

Listen to the tune on Track 35. Point to each note as you hear it.

Match that tune

Listen to the three tunes on tracks 36–38. Can you match them to
these three tunes?

The answers are given on page 64.

Write that tune

Covering up the music above, listen to each tune on tracks 36, 37 and
38 (each is played three times, beginning with the pulse). Try writing the
first two bars of each from memory. After you've written it down, hear
it internally, sing it out loud and then compare it to the track. They all
begin on the note C.

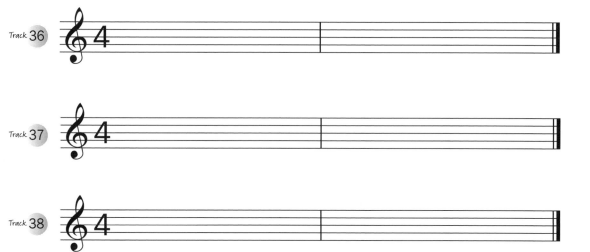

More markings

There are even more markings on music to indicate how you should play or sing.

> **Tempo markings** tell us the speed of a tune and are shown by a word (or words) at the beginning of the piece just above the first bar. They are often in Italian (because Italy was where music notation was born). This will affect the speed of your **pulse**. Here are two common tempo markings:
>
> **Adagio** which means slow
>
> **Allegro** which means lively

> **Articulation markings** show whether the notes are joined smoothly or detached. We use **slurs** ⌒ to join up notes, making them flow smoothly. If notes are not joined by a slur they are slightly more detached.

Prepare, hear and sing these tunes in the usual way, thinking about the different tempo and articulation for each.

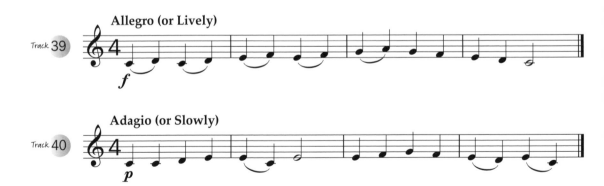

30

Reading all the markings

Prepare these final two tunes in Part 1 in the usual way. The first note
can be heard on track 5. Set up an appropriate pulse (a faster one for
41 and a slower one for 42) then hear the tune in your head, including
the dynamic and articulation markings. Then (still tapping the pulse)
sing each out loud. Finally, listen to them on tracks 41 and 42.

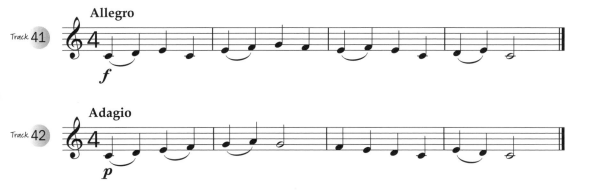

Track 41

Track 42

The final music in Part 1 ...

... is for you to compose. Write your own piece using all the ingredients
you know, then read and sing it with understanding and confidence.
These are the ingredients to choose from:

- Tempo: **Allegro** (lively) or **Adagio** (slow)

- Notes: C, D, E, F, G and A

- Movement: repeat a note, move by step or the interval of a third

- Rhythms: ♩, ♩ and ♩ and their rests

- Dynamics: *f* and *p*

- Articulation: detached notes (unmarked) and slurs

Part 2

When we read music we hear sounds. The music on the page tells us the pitch of the sound (how high or low it is) and the duration of the sound (how short or long it is).

And that's just about it!

There are various other markings that can help us with the way we play or sing those notes, but it's mainly about pitch and duration.

Music notation doesn't tell us which finger to use, or which button, key, ring, valve (or anything else) we should press (or do anything to).

It tells us what the music sounds like. And we are now well on the way to being able to look at music notation and have a good idea what it's going to sound like.

And as we learn to play an instrument or sing, we simply learn how to bring those symbols to life.

Completing the scale

Here are all the notes we know so far. Listen to track 5 for the first note (C). Tap a bar of crotchets (quietly) and hear the pattern in your head. Then, keeping the pulse going, sing the notes out loud (to their letter names or any sound you like).

Now listen to the pattern on track 43.

All those notes belong to the **scale of C major**. Let's complete the scale: here's what it looks like with the final two notes (taking us up to the next C):

> Notice the **direction of the note stems**. They fall downwards from the note head for those last two notes: this is just to make them look neater and easier to read. The stem direction has no effect on rhythm or pitch.

Listen to track 5 for the note C and, tapping four introductory beats, hear the whole scale in your head, then sing it out loud. You've read and sung your first scale, and enjoyed it too, I hope: scales are friendly and useful patterns.

Through the keyhole

> If a piece or song uses the notes of C major we say it's in the **key** of C major. It often begins and ends on the note C, too.

The next tunes are all in the **key** of C major. They use ingredients we've learnt about so far. Prepare them in the usual way:

- Look at each phrase and get a general idea of what it says. Look for patterns and describe the patterns in words.

- Tap four beats then (continuing to tap the pulse) read and hear the phrase *internally*, singing each note to its pitch name or any sound you like. You can hear the first note on Track 5.

- Continue to tap the pulse and sing the phrase out loud.

Now listen to them on tracks 45–49.

Mind the gap

Every key is made up of the notes of its scale. There's another useful pattern connected with each key. It is made up of three notes so is called a **triad** (like *tri*angle or *tri*cycle). A triad is made up of the 1st, 3rd and 5th notes of the scale. In C major they are:

Track 50

C   E   G

Each note in a triad jumps over a note.

Listen to Track 5 for the pitch of the note C and then:

● Sing the C

● Hear the D in your head

● Sing the E

● Hear the F in your head

● Sing the G

Now sing C – E – G.

Listen to track 50 to hear these notes.

The importance of triads

Triads are often used in airports or stations as the call to attention before an announcement. It's an important pattern. Here are some phrases which contain triad patterns. Prepare and have fun with each one in the usual way:

And here's a traditional folk song that uses lots of triads:

Setting the tone

When we go up or down the notes of a scale you may think that the distance between each note is the same. In fact some next-door notes are closer than others! There are two different distances between next-door notes.

Read this pattern and sense the distance from one note to the next on track 57:

Track 57

The distance between the C — D and D – E are the same – it is called a **tone**. But did you notice the distance between the E and F was a little smaller? It's called a **semitone**.

The notes of a major scale are always made up of the same pattern of tones and semitones. Here they are. Read the pattern, listening really thoughtfully to the distance between each note – both internally and when you sing it out loud.

Track 58

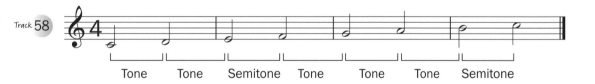

Tone   Tone   Semitone   Tone   Tone   Tone   Semitone

Listen to the scale on track 58.

At the sharp end

Although we find lots of different keys in music, there are only really two main patterns: major keys and minor keys. And what's more, all major keys sound the same, and all minor keys sound the same. We know C major already, so let's look at the **key of G major**.

The **G major scale** begins on G. To satisfy the correct pattern of tones and semitones for a major key we need to raise the seventh note by a semitone. We do this with a symbol called a **sharp**: ♯

Here's the scale of G major with a sharp sign attached to the seventh note, making it an *F sharp*. Listen to track 59 to hear the note G and then hear the scale in your head. If your voice goes high enough you can sing it out loud. Listen to track 60 to hear the scale.

Track 59

Track 60

At the flat end

Some keys have notes which need to be lowered to fit the pattern of tones and semitones for a major key. In the key of **F major** we need to lower the fourth note by a semitone. We do this with a symbol called a **flat**: ♭ Here's the scale of F major with the flat attached to the fourth note, making it *B flat*. Listen to track 61 to hear the note F and then hear the scale in your head. Again, if your voice goes high enough, you can sing it out loud:

Track 61

Track 62

If a piece or song is written in the **key of G major** (where all Fs have to be F sharps), rather than write a sharp sign before each F we use a clever short cut. We put a sharp on the F line at the beginning of the stave (after the clef) which indicates that all the Fs should be sung or played as F sharps. We call this a **key signature**.

Here's the key signature of G major. (The sharp symbol is always shown on the higher F.)

Here's a scale of G major ascending and descending. Listen to track 59 to hear a G then read it, hearing it internally.

Track 63

Listen to Track 63 to hear the scale.

Listen to track 59 again to hear a G, then read the triad pattern, hear it internally then sing the notes out loud.

Track 64

Now listen to it on track 64.

Here are some well-known tunes written in G major. Can you read and recognise them?

Track 65

Track 66

There's a new leap in the next tune between the first two notes. It's the leap between the 1st and the 5th notes of the scale (or between the 1st and 3rd note of the triad). Can you recognise the tune?

Track 67

This eight-bar melody is the first part of a gospel hymn that has become a famous jazz number. Can you spot a triad?

Track 68

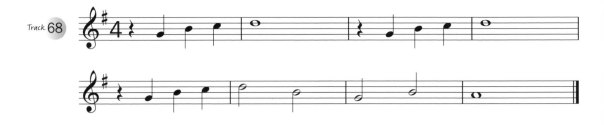

You can listen to them on tracks 65–68. The tunes are named on page 64.

Key signature of F major

Here's the key signature of F major:

And the triad pattern:

Track 69

Listen to track 61 to hear an F then read the triad, hearing it internally.
Now sing the notes out loud and then listen to the pattern.

Read these phrases in F major, preparing them in the usual way. Can
you spot any F major triad patterns?

Track 70

Track 71

Track 72

Did you notice the repeated pattern in bars 1, 2 and 3 of the last
phrase? Spotting these patterns will help your music reading. Listen to
these phrases on tracks 70–72.

Turn up the bass

If you play the piano you'll know that it is the higher notes that are written on a stave with a treble clef, which are generally played by the right hand.

So we also need a way of writing lower notes – notes played (usually) by a pianist's left hand or on lower-pitched instruments like the cello, bassoon and tuba. For this we use the **bass clef**. Here it is:

The bass clef was originally called the **F clef** because it looked a little like an old-fashioned letter F and because the line between those two dots is where the note F sits. Let's start by seeing where the note A lives in the bass clef:

Track 73

A

It sits in the bottom space and we'll see why that is important on the next page. Listen to track 73 to hear this note, then look at the note and hear the A in your head for 4 beats. Track 74 gives the note C: listen to it and repeat the process with C on the bass clef.

Track 74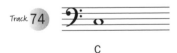

C

Reading the bass clef ...

...is no different from reading the treble clef: the notes are just in different places. If you put the treble and bass staves together it creates the **great stave**. This shows why the notes are named in the order they are. You don't need to learn where all the notes are, it will happen gradually as you read, sing and play more music.

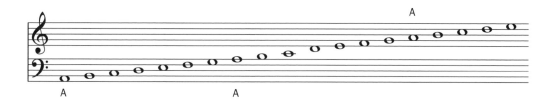

Study the great stave for a moment and think about where the notes are (remembering that we only use the letter names A to G). Look at where the As are: they are useful landmark notes.

Let's read some bass clef phrases in C major. Listen to track 74 for your C and then read each of these tunes. Prepare each in the usual way, ending with singing them out loud. (You can still sing these if you have high voice, you'll just sing them an octave* higher.) Then listen to them on tracks 75–77.

*An octave is an interval of 8 notes, which takes you to the same note within your vocal range.

Track 78 Here are some phrases in G major. Low G is written on the bottom line of the stave (below the A on the first space). All these phrases begin on that G. Listen to it on track 78 then prepare and read each phrase in the usual way.

And now for some phrases in F major. Low F is written below the bottom line of the stave. Listen to Track 83 for an F and then to tracks 84–87 to hear each phrase.

Time to compose (again)

Write your own phrases in the bass clef – two in G major and two in F major. Use whichever ingredients you'd like to, but always begin and end on the **key-note** (the first note of the scale) and check that each bar adds up to four beats.

Try to hear each piece in your head as you are writing it. Give each a title.

The key-signatures have been put in for you.

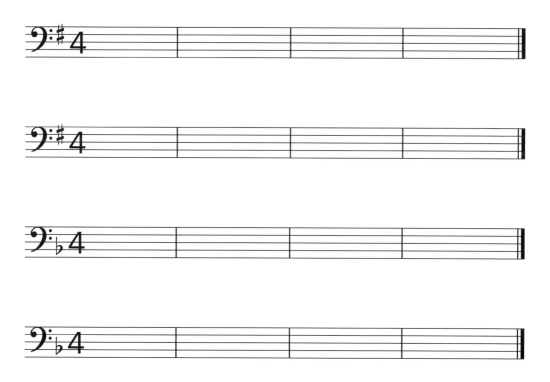

If you have a friend with a bass-clef instrument ask them to play your pieces for you.

A minor thought

Music comes in two different kinds of keys – major and minor ones. So far all the music we have been reading has been in major keys.

Major and minor keys sound different. As teachers have told their pupils for generations, music in major keys sounds cheerful and happy and music in **minor keys** sounds doleful and sad.

Every major key has a **relative minor key** – a close relative like a brother or sister. Both use the same key signature (the sharps or flats at the start of a piece) and very similar notes.

C major has no sharps or flats. The minor scale that has no sharps or flats is **A minor**. So A minor is the **relative minor** of C major (and C major is the **relative major** of A minor).

If we build a scale on A using just white notes, we create the **natural minor**. Listen to it a few times on Track 88. Notice the character – particularly how it differs from a major scale.

Track 88

There are other forms of the minor scale to learn about, but the natural minor is a good place to start.

All of a quaver

So far we have met crotchets (1-beat notes), minims (2-beat notes) and semibreves (4-beat notes). We're going to meet a shorter note value now – two will fit into one crotchet. This is called a **quaver** (or **eighth note**).

Tap this line of crotchets, counting the beat numbers as you do:

Still tapping the crotchets, add the sound 'uh' between each number, spacing each number and the in-between sound very evenly:

Still tapping the crotchets, replace the numbers with the sound 'uh':

What you are hearing are quavers.

Have a quaver

A single **quaver** looks like this: ♪

If we write them by hand, they usually look more like this: ♪

Two quavers are joined together like this: ♫

Four quavers together are written like this: ♫♫

The word **quaver** actually comes from an old thirteenth-century word meaning to 'tremble' or 'sing in trills'.

Here's what that last bar of music on the previous page looks like written out in quavers:

1   uh   2   uh   3   uh   4   uh

Tap a bar of crotchets and then read the bar, counting the notes as '1 uh 2 uh' etc. Then read again, hearing each quaver as an 'uh'.

Here's a tune to read. Begin by tapping a bar of crotchets (1-beat notes) and then hear just the rhythm in your head. Next hear the rhythm and pitch together (listen to track 1 for a C), then sing it out loud. Listen to it on track 89.

Track 89

Here are some tunes to read which include quavers. Prepare them in
the usual way:

Track 90

Track 91

Track 92

Here's a well-known song to read. It begins on the fifth note of the C
major scale. Can you recognise it? (See page 64 for the answer.)

Track 93

Allegro

Listen to Track 93 to hear it.

Markings galore

We've met two tempo (speed) markings (*adagio* and *allegro*) already, two dynamic markings (𝒇 and 𝒑) and slurs. We're going to meet some more of these useful markings that tell us how to make the music sound more colourful and interesting.

> Two important markings are **crescendo** and **diminuendo**. *Crescendo* means getting gradually louder and *diminuendo* means getting gradually quieter. Sometimes they are marked using the complete word; sometimes by an abbreviation (*cresc.* or *dim.*) and sometimes by what musicians refer to as '**hairpins**':
>
> crescendo   diminuendo

Here is a simple phrase. Read it and hear the notes getting louder and then quieter. Sing it too if you like (listen to the start of track 94 to hear the note):

Track 94

Listen to track 94 to hear it.

Short and sweet

> If we want notes to be short and sprightly we mark them with a dot under or over the note head – this is known as **staccato**. The word is Italian and means 'detached'. A staccato note sounds shorter than its full written value.

Listen to a C (track 5) and then hear this scale of C major with each note staccato. There's a new tempo (speed) marking too (which probably doesn't need much explanation!).

Read the next tune with all its markings. Tap an introductory four beats (the pulse) and then, continuing to tap the pulse, read the music:

Track 95

Did you recognise the tune? Listen to track 95 to hear it.

Here's a nursery rhyme and street cry connected to a tasty spiced bun. Prepare it in the usual way. It begins on the third note of the C major scale (the second note of the triad).

Track 96

May I have this dance?

So far all the music we've been reading in this book has had four beats in a bar. But music can have different numbers of beats in a bar. We're going to look at music with **3 beats** in a bar (which some call waltz time).

Let's count in three first. Using your watch or time-telling digital device, count the pattern below, with '1' on each second:

123**1**23**1**23**1**23

Here's a phrase with the same counting pattern:

Track 97

Listen to track 5 for the C and then read it. Listen again and tap the notes on the page with your finger as you hear them – tap the first note in each bar more strongly than the others. Now sing it out loud.

In most music there is also a lower number in a **time signature** (the symbol, usually two numbers, at the start of a piece showing how many beats there are in a bar). This lower number is a code for the type of beats that we are counting. We're only using bars of crotchet beats in this book and the code for crotchet beats is 4.

$\frac{4}{4}$ = 4 crotchet beats in each bar.

$\frac{3}{4}$ = 3 crotchet beats in each bar.

Here's a well-known folk song in 3-time to read. The first leap is from the first to the fifth note of the scale (the bottom to the top note of the triad). Your preparatory count in will be three taps for music in three time. There's also a new dynamic marking: *mp* (from the Italian *mezzo piano*) which means fairly quiet.

Track 98

Did you recognise it? Listen to it on track 98.

Here are some more tunes in 3-time for you to read. Don't forget all the markings and enjoy the musical colour. It's like reading words (silently) with lots of expression.

Listen to track 5 for the first note (C), track 59 for the G and track 83 for the low F.

Track 99

Track 100

Track 101

53

Jigsaw waltz

Here are four bars. Read each bar and then have a go at creating a
four-bar waltz by choosing an order and writing them out below. There
are two empty staves for you to try different combinations.

Do you prefer one more than the other? Why?

Waltz without faultz

Have a go at writing your own waltz! Just make sure that each bar adds up to three beats. There are many note-value combinations – here are a few:

- Three crotchets

- A crotchet and a minim

- One crotchet and four quavers

- Two crotchets and two quavers

You could write in C, G or F major and in the treble or bass clef (both are ready for you below). Write a waltz that you can play or sing. Whichever key you decide on, make the first and last note the key-note (the first note of the scale). Sprinkle your waltz with lots of musical markings.

Louder please!

We've met three different dynamic markings so far: ***p***, ***mp*** and ***f***.

There are six markings commonly used in music*:

> ***pp*** (***pianissimo***) means very quiet
>
> ***p*** (***piano***) means quiet
>
> ***mp*** (***mezzo piano***) means moderately quiet
>
> ***mf*** (***mezzo forte***) means moderately loud
>
> ***f*** (***forte***) means loud
>
> ***ff*** (***fortissimo***) means very loud

* If you don't count the Russian composer, Tchaikovsky, who liked to use rather eccentric dynamic markings such as ***pppppp***. You can see this in bar 160 of the first movement of his sixth symphony.

Hearing dynamics in your head

When reading music internally it's not that easy to make much contrast between dynamic markings (imagine a very loud sound… then a very quiet one…). Here are two tunes to hear internally. Read them through, imagining the various dynamics as effectively as you can (listen to track 5 for the first note, C):

Track **102**

Track **103**

If you can sing or play these pieces, then it's much easier to bring the dynamic markings to life. Have a go at singing them out loud and then listen to them on tracks 102–103.

Pause occasionally in everyday life and think what dynamic level particular sounds are: the telephone ringing, a dog barking, an annoying hum from the fridge, water filling the bath. Does your position and distance from the sound make a difference? This will increase your awareness of dynamic levels.

Parliamo Italiano?*

Most musical markings are written in the lovely Italian language. They convey many different types of musical information and there are a great many of them! When you come across one you don't know, you can look it up on the internet or in a book of Italian musical terms.

Here are the main categories which use Italian terms, with a couple of examples of each:

- Musical forms (*aria* and *concerto*)

- Musical instruments (*piano* and *piccolo*)

- Voices (*soprano* and *alto*)

- Tempo (*andante* and *allegretto*)

- Tempo alterations (*accelerando* and *rallentando*)

- Moods (*dolce* and *espressivo*)

- Directions (*legato* and *vibrato*)

- Technical instructions (*con sordino* and *pizzicato*)

* **Can we speak Italian?**

The beautiful art of sub-division (and a new note)

We've learnt the following note lengths so far:

- Semibreve (four beats)
- Minim (two beats)
- Crotchet (one beat)
- Quaver (half a crotchet beat)

We're going to look at one more note length. But first – what is half a circle called? Answer: a semicircle.

Two of these new notes fit into a quaver – they are equal to half a quaver. So what are they called?

Semiquavers (or **sixteenth notes**).

They look like this:

Four joined together look like this:

Four of them fit into one crotchet. So it's time to try some sub-dividing:

- Tap a fairly slow crotchet pulse (no more than one per second).
- In your head, hear each tap sub-divided into two (perhaps by inserting the sound 'uh'). You're hearing quavers. Two quavers for each crotchet beat.
- Now, in your head, hear each tap sub-divided into four. You're hearing semiquavers.

Putting it all together

This is the family of note lengths so far and how they are related:

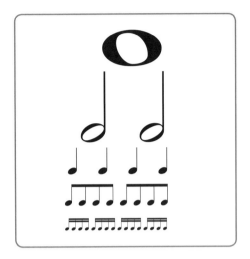

Here are three tunes to read that include some semiquavers.

Listen to track 5 for the note C.

Then listen to these tunes.

Two for the price of one

Pianists usually have to read two lines of music at the same time, one line for the right hand and one for the left. Conductors sometimes have to read forty lines at the same time! You don't have to be a superhero to do this! Read what's in the next box in a quick glance:

> I'm
> reading
> this

You read it and it wasn't particularly difficult. Have another look at those words. Can you see them as a single pattern rather than three individual words? In fact, the eye can take in more than you might think. Try reading these two lines simultaneously:

> I'm reading this line of words
> I'm reading this line of words too

If you are a pianist or a conductor, or would like to develop the skill of reading more complex music from notation, the answer is simply to practise! Read music on a regular basis and you'll become as fluent (and accurate) at reading it as you are at reading these words.

So you can read music!

Once you really *understand* the ingredients (note lengths, pitch and the various other markings), looking at music and knowing what it sounds like will begin to develop quickly.

You'll find sight-reading or sight-singing much easier and you'll learn new pieces and songs on your own more quickly. You'll be able to join orchestras, choirs and other groups with confidence, knowing that reading the music will not be a problem!

In this book we've learnt the basics of reading music. You can now look at music notation and know what it sounds like. If you play an instrument or sing, remember that when you look at the notation what you are seeing is a picture of the sound. Your job is to turn what you can see and hear in your head into lovely music.

Glossary of terms

Adagio tempo marking meaning slow

Allegro tempo marking meaning lively

Articulation markings indicate whether notes are joined or detached

Bar short units into which music is split

Barline a line across the stave which breaks the music into bars

Bass clef 𝄢 symbol at the start of the stave which tells you which (left-hand) notes to play or read

Beat a basic unit of time; what we count

Clef symbol at the start of a stave which tells you which notes to play or read

Crescendo getting gradually louder

Crotchet (or **quarter note**) ♩ a one-beat note (or rest)

Diminuendo getting gradually quieter

Duration the length of time for which a note is played or sung

Dynamics markings which convey how loud or quiet music should be

F clef original name for the bass clef

Flat ♭ a symbol which lowers a note by a semitone

Forte (*f*) dynamic level meaning loud

Fortissimo dynamic level meaning very loud

Great stave when the treble and bass clef staves are put together (usually in piano music)

Hairpin name given to *crescendo* and *diminuendo* signs ⟨───── ─────⟩

Interval distance or gap between the pitch of notes

Key defines music based on the notes of a particular scale

Key-note the first note of a scale

Key signature the sharps or flats at the start of a piece which indicate which key it is in

Major key a pattern of tones and semitones that sounds cheerful and happy

Measure US term for a bar

Mezzo forte dynamic level meaning moderately loud

Mezzo piano dynamic level meaning moderately quiet

Minor key a pattern of tones and semitones which sounds doleful and sad

Metronome device which produces regular beats

Minim (or **half note**) ♩ a two-beat note (or rest)

Note musical symbol showing pitch and duration

Notehead the oval part of a note

Quaver two of these make one crotchet

Phrase a short pattern or group of notes in music

Piano (p) dynamic level meaning quiet

Pianissimo dynamic level meaning very quiet

Pitch how high or low the sound is

Pulse regular beat in music (like a heartbeat)

Relative major the major key which shares the same key signature as the minor

Relative minor the minor key which shares the same key signature as the major

Rest indicates silence in music

Rhythm the arrangement of musical sounds according to duration

Scale a sequence of 8 notes which move up or down in step

Second the interval (or gap) between next-door notes

Semibreve (or **whole note**) ○ a four-beat note (or rest)

Semiquaver four of these make one crotchet

Semitone the smallest distance in pitch between two notes

Sharp ♯ a symbol which raises a note by a semitone

Slur ⌣ shows that notes should connect smoothly

Staccato a dot above or below a note-head indicates a short, detached note

Stave five lines on which music is written

Stem the stalk of a musical note

Tempo the speed of music

Tempo markings word (or words) which describe the speed of a tune

Tone the distance in pitch between notes; made up of two semitones

Third an interval (or gap) of 3 note names between notes

Time signature symbol which shows you how many beats are in each bar

Treble clef 𝄞 symbol at the start of the stave which tells you which (right-hand) notes to play

Triad the 1st, 3rd and 5th notes of a scale

Answers

p.21: Frère Jacques, Jingle Bells, Mary Had A Little Lamb, Ode To Joy

p.25: Long Long Ago

p.28: Au Clair De La Lune

p.29: No.1 = Track 38, No.2 = Track 36, No.3 = Track 37

p.40: Au Clair De La Lune, Merrily We Roll Along, Twinkle Twinkle Little Star, When The Saints

p.49: This Old Man

p.51: Pease Pudding Hot, Hot Cross Buns

p.53: Lavender's Blue